Penny Stocks:

A Quick and Easy Guide for Beginners to Start Investing

Pete Manlow

Additionally, the information in the following pages is intended only for informational purposes and should thus be thought of as universal. As befitting its nature, it is presented without assurance regarding its prolonged validity or interim quality. Trademarks that are mentioned are done without written consent and can in no way be considered an endorsement from the trademark holder.

Table of Contents

Introduction

Congratulations on buying *Penny Stocks: A Quick and Easy Guide for Beginners to Start Investing* and thank you for doing so. When it comes to taking the first step to expanding your investment portfolio there are few better ways of going about doing so than via investing in the stock market. While there are plenty of investment avenues to choose from, penny stocks offer up many unique benefits that make them desirable regardless of whether you are looking to invest in your very first stock or if you are a seasoned veteran looking to try something new.

They are not without their own unique drawbacks as well, however, which is why the following chapters will discuss everything you need to know to get started as quickly and efficiently as possible, beginning with a complete breakdown of what a penny stock is exactly and how it differs from stock of a more traditional type. Next you will learn to create a personalized trading plan that can take advantage of all that penny stocks have to offer. With a plan firmly in place you will then learn about the various different trading styles that are typically associated with penny stocks and how to know which is for you.

With the fundamentals out of the way, you will then learn about the two types of analysis that are right for any situation, both technical and fundamental, and how to know which one you will use in any given situation. Finally, you will learn various tips and tricks to ensuring your time trading penny stocks is profitable as well as common mistakes that many new penny stock traders make and how to avoid them.

There are plenty of books on this subject on the market, thanks again for choosing this one! Every effort was made to ensure it is full of as much useful information as possible, please enjoy!

Chapter 1:
Understanding Penny Stocks

Everyone has heard of the major stock exchanges where ownership shares of major companies are bought and sold and the fortunes of day traders are won and lost. In fact, these concepts are such a staunch pillar of the economy that most people have likely never stopped to think why companies decide to start offering public stock in the first place.

The fact of the matter is that selling stock is one way that companies can generate investment revenue, either to continue their current operations or to fund new ones. While major companies have less of a direct need for an influx of this type of capital, for smaller businesses it can be their shot at the big time. Along these same lines, while large companies can expect to be listed on the major exchanges, small companies looking to go public for the first time are typically relegated to the minor leagues of the stock market which is where penny stocks come into the picture.

The name penny stocks is the general classification given to a wide variety of stocks that can actually trade at anything less than $5.00 per share. In addition to sticking to smaller amounts per share, these types of stocks are going to be able to first be listed after a much less strict overall overview process than they would with the larger exchanges. This means that the company could be completely sound, just untested, or it could be barely more than an idea without even a working business plan, which is where the risk comes in to balance out the potential reward. The potential for reward is great, however, as the low price of penny stocks means that you could easily pick up enough shares to see a significant return from a relatively small amount of positive movement.

While the reward may be great, the specter hanging over all penny stocks is the fact that a majority of them ultimately end up going belly up before they have generated any sort of substantial return for their investors. Despite this fact, the draw of penny stocks is readily apparent when you look at what the estimated return is when compared with that of a similar stock from one of the major markets. As an example, if you have $1,000 to invest and choose to do so in a mundane stock that generates an average rate of return of 10 percent then after 50 years you can expect to make roughly $120,000 for your troubles. In that same period of time, however, if you manage to successfully invest in penny stocks then the total you could make over this same period of time doubles to 20 percent or nearly $10,000,000 total.

Market capitalization

Many of the companies in this tier tend to offer goods as opposed to services and they may even be at such an early point that they can still be considered in the startup phase which is why they are equally as likely to fail as they are too succeed, even with the influx of investor capital that being listed on a stock exchange provides. As such, the first step to determining if a penny stock is ultimately going to be worth your time is to consider what is known as market capitalization.

Market capitalization is a basic mathematical equation that lets those who are interested in investing in penny stocks determine, more or less, how financially sound a company is likely to be and is the same formula that is used by financial institutions to determine loans. To understand how it works, consider the following example: Assume a company has issued 1,000 shares of stock, this includes everything including those that are owned by private individuals and those owned by the company itself. If that is the case, and assuming that each share is worth $1, then the worth of that company's stock, also known as the market cap maxes out at $1,000 total. Alternatively, you can think of the market cap as the product of the number of shares and the price of each.

With the market cap in mind you will then be able to determine how much other investors will likely be willing to pay to purchase a single share of the company and how much the company would be able to earn from selling all their currently existing stock. Companies whose stock exists on a major exchange are going to have a much higher overall market cap, which will, in turn make it much easier to get credit from a financial institution as it is unlikely that their stock price is going to change drastically in a short period of time.

It is important to keep in mind that market capitalization functions much different for major companies than it does for those that earn the classification penny stocks. Major companies are unlikely to be borrowing against what they market capitalization turns out to be out of necessity, while penny stock companies are sure to do so almost immediately. While major companies are likely to borrow against their market cap when it comes time to generate a new product line, it is rarely the life or death situation that it is with penny stocks. Furthermore, the sheer number of assets that major companies have readily available puts the overall relevance of the market capitalization in a different perspective.

The goal then is to choose penny stocks whose companies have enough market capitalization to ensure that they remain in existence long enough for their stock price to increase to the point that you can sell it to make a profit. An increase in the penny stock's market capitalization not only means that it is likely going to have an increased stock price, it is going to be easier to sell as well.

A needle in haystack

In addition to the fact that many new companies are untested and are just as likely to see failure as they are success, the other greatest hurdle you will need to overcome with penny stocks is the fact that there are just so many too choose from. This means that not only do the companies that you choose to invest in need to beat the odds and succeed in their chosen field, they also need to beat out all of their immediate competitors as well. These are companies that are looking to compete on a national or international stage which means that before you invest you are going to know just what type of competition that you are dealing with.

This is much more of an issue when it comes to penny stocks, simply because most of the companies listed there are relatively limited to only a handful of true competitors. When you compare this to the average number of competitors that most penny stock companies are dealing with on a regular basis the competition is several times more intense. As such, you are going to want to take the time to research not just the company you are interested in investing in, but the entire field that it is a part of.

Ask the right questions

Finally, when it comes to considering specific penny stocks, it is important to ask yourself why the company you are looking at specifically is interested in becoming listed on the penny stock exchange. The answer to this question is likely less straightforward than it seems as new companies have more options when it comes to financing now than they have at any other point in history. The companies you are interested in should be the ones looking to gain prestige on a larger stage, not the ones that are scrambling for cash to salvage what could very well be a sinking ship.

Likewise, you are typically going to want to avoid technology companies because profitable options are even more difficult to identify correctly in that industry than they are elsewhere. This is especially true for many of the most popular websites out there today from Groupon, to Twitter to Tinder, none of which manage to turn much, if any, profit. With that being said, it is clear that these companies and those like them have no difficulty finding investors which means that if you are going to go down this road the best indicator of whether other investors are going to jump on board is the size of the active user base the company currently boasts. The more users, the higher the valuation of the company's stock is going to be, it is as simple as that.

Chapter 2:
Create A Personalized Trading Plan

Before you can go ahead and get down to picking out the penny stocks you want to invest in, it is important that you have a personalized trading plan already established so you are sure to know exactly what it is that you are looking for. The simple truth of the matter is that you can in no way expect to find trading success in the long term if you aren't playing to your own unique strengths and weaknesses right from the word go. While you may be tempted to skip this section in an effort to get to trading as quickly as possible, you will find that a more generalized trading plan is going to ultimately be nowhere near as effective in either the short or the long term.

Consider your familiarity with trading: When it comes to creating a trading plan that is sure to lead to success, the first thing that you will want to consider is your overall familiarity with the ins and outs of trading in general, and higher risk trading in particular. The greater your overall experience level, the more ambitious your plan, and your trades can be, but there is no shame is sticking with the basics if you are just getting started overall. When it comes to determining your personal skill level, it is important to be honest with yourself as overestimating your abilities is only going to come back to haunt you later on when you end up in over your head with more than you can realistically afford to lose on the line.

While working to determine your overall trading baseline, it is also important to determine your general strengths and weaknesses when it comes to trading as a whole. Special consideration should then be given to the ease at which you remain calm under pressure and are able to stick to a plan even when you feel your emotions pulling you in another direction. Again, it is important to be true to yourself when determining these specifics as this is not some test you can fail, it is an assessment to help your trading plan fit you like a glove; if you create a false baseline the only person who will be hurt by the truth is you.

Think about your current situation: When it comes to planning out your trading goals it is important to consider anything else that you currently have going on in your life that you know will keep you from trading either as much as you would like or to the degree that you are aiming for. While you may find that a goal which is a little out of reach can be used as a motivating force, the truth of the matter is that if you are not realistic about your limitations the plan you come up with won't be of any real use in a practical setting.

Other obstacles in your path can be things like financial limitations or limitations on your time, the specifics don't particularly matter, all that matters is that you are aware of them so you can work in ways to get around them into the very heart of your plan. While facing your limitations might be daunting, the fact of the matter is that doing so will not only make it more likely that you will succeed, it will increase the amount you are likely to bank every step of the way. Remember, forewarned is forearmed.

Consider your tolerance for risk: If you are interested in penny stocks then you are likely already more tolerant of risk

13

than many investors. With that being said, there is still a spectrum to consider when it comes to how much risk you find acceptable when it comes to putting your money where your mouth is. The amount risk that is the right amount of risk is going to be different for every person which is why it is so important to consider how you feel about high risk and high reward (for penny stocks) situations. In order to determine the right amount of risk for you, the first thing that you will want to do is consider the capital you are going to have when you first start out trading. Once you have a firm amount in mind it is equally important to consider how long it took you to save up the amount of money in question as you would naturally treat $1,000 differently if it took you six months to save as opposed to a few weeks to throw together.

If you are using an amount of money that was relatively easy for you to put together, then the amount of risk you are adding to the situation is going to be fairly low, while if you are putting your life savings on the line then your overall inherent risk is going to much higher. It doesn't how much of a starter fund you have prepared for yourself, you are always going to want to take special care to never put more into a trade than you can afford to lose. A reliable way to ensure that this is case is to create a rule that says you will never put more than 5 percent of your total trading fund into a single trade as a way of minimizing any inherent risk in the trading process as much ass possible.

Additionally, it is important to ensure that you never enter into any trade without a relative level of certainty that you will make at least three times as much back on the trade in profit as you are risking buying into the trade in the first place, after all fees have been taken into account. The easiest way to ensure that this is the case is to start with the total amount you expect to make in the exchange and then divide that number by the amount it will cost you to buy-in in the first place. If you end up with a number that is somewhere north of 3 then you can move forward with confidence assuming your reasoning behind your profit numbers are sound. This number is what is known as the reward/risk ratio and using it is crucial when it comes to trading successfully in the long term.

In addition to the amount of capital that you are going to be able to dedicate to investing in penny stocks, you are also going to want to seriously consider how much time you are going to spend making trades each week. With that in mind, you will then want to consider what your goals are when it comes to making a profit. With a general level of profit in mind, the next thing that you will need to do is determine if the amount of capital you have available, along with the amount of time you to dedicate to trading can realistically equal the amount of profit you are hoping to obtain. If the numbers do not add up, you can change one or more of the variables involved but ultimately the three amounts need to be in agreement.

Remember, when it comes to shortening the amount of time you plan on trading, without decreasing profits, you are counting on risk to fill in the difference. It is important to only do this sparingly as penny stocks are inherently one of the riskier investment types which can lead to larger payouts but also to greater losses.

Know what you are in for: When you are calculating the amount of time that you will need to dedicate to trading to ensure a steady profit, it is important to also factor in how long it is going to take you to properly prepare for each day of trading. Specifically, you will want to ensure that you have plenty of time each morning before the market opens to research the current state of things, doing so will help you to maximize any advantages your plan might provide you with for the day and prevent you from being surprised and making decisions based on outdate information.

In addition to preparing each day, you are also going to need to allot time to keeping abreast of various important dates related to the industries of the penny stocks that you tend to favor. Earnings reports of one sort or another are virtually guaranteed to affect the market you are working in and the only way that you will know to be prepared for it is if you constantly keep abreast of the state of things, even if you are not actively trading at the moment.

Set your limits: In order to create a reliable trading strategy it is important to start by considering how much profit you are willing to accept and what you are willing to do in order to protect that much profit. Specifically, this means you will want to consider how much movement by the stock in question you will be willing to allow before cashing out. The type of movement that you will want to consider in this instance is when a stock that has moved in a positive direction then drops all the way down so that it is now below even the price it started out. This state is referred to as being out of the money and when a stock, especially a penny stock, reaches this point it is extremely unlikely that it is going to rebound to the point that it is profitable once again.

When a stock that you have a personal attachment too drops out of the money it can be natural to want to hold on to it until the point at which it rebounds. This is akin to throwing good money after bad, however, and it is a much better idea to instead set a stop loss, or an automated order to sell, once the stock reaches the point where it is out of the money. Stop losses only work on stocks that are not oscillating so wildly that they drop from one extreme to another multiple times in a matter of minutes as otherwise they will trigger during the first oscillation.

Secondary stop losses can also be set when you feel as though a penny stock is on a strong positive upswing but still wish to ensure that all of the current gains are not lost should things swing back in the other direction. This is when you will want to utilize a price target which is how much you are going to be satisfied making and walking away from the trade happy. Your first stop loss should be set at this point with a secondary stop loss set significantly higher to account for the eventual backslide while still keeping a majority of your profits intact.

Much as when it comes to determining the right amount of risk, determining the best strategy is going to comes down to personal preference and proclivities as well as how closely you plan on monitoring every trade. As such, the specific details of what your exit plan aren't necessarily important, what is important is that you take into account all of your personal preferences, including how much risk you are willing to accept, and have a firm idea of the specifics before you get started and then stick to your guns, even if your emotions are raging and you have a strong desire to change horses mid-stream.

Choose an entry point: Once you have a clear idea of how much profit you are going to shoot for, you will want to take into account the types of trends you are going to look for when it comes to picking out new penny stocks to invest in. Choosing the right point to jump in on a new penny stock is going to be a personal preference based on risk tolerance as well earnings goals and personal time frame. Only by setting a standard that is rigorous enough to weed out the chaff, while still being realistic enough to provide you with enough choice in the matter to ensure your success. The goal here should be to decide on a specific set of details that you look for before choosing an entry point and then using them every single time. Only by developing a strict level of consistency will you ever hope to see the results you are dreaming of.

Establish clear goals: In order to ensure you have created a beneficial plan, it is important to compare your theoretical results with your overall goals both in the short and in the long term in order to guarantee they mesh properly. The trading goals that you set for yourself should be realistic as well as attainable based on any limiting factors in your life; they should also be attainable as if you feel as though your goals are forever out of reach then this will ultimately have a negative effect on your motivation.

What' s more, you will want to do what you can to set goals that are as specific as possible as goals that are clearly stated are much easier to pursue in the long term which means they are more likely to actually build to completion. Additionally, being specific means your goals should have clear instances of success and failure to keep you firmly on track. Along similar lines, it is important to always have a timeline in which to meet or exceed your goals to always keep you motivated to strive for the next deadline. Prior to setting a long-term goal for your penny stock investing it is important to take into account all of the related logistics to ensure that the deadlines you do come up with are ultimately reasonable and prevent you from accidentally doing more harm than good.

Keep track the right way: It doesn't matter if you have been trading penny stocks for two months or twenty years, if you aren't keeping track of your failure and success rate then you know will have no way of knowing if the primary trading plan that you are using is worth the metaphorical paper it is written on. This is especially true when you are just starting out as individual successes or failures still represent so much of your overall trade experience that a handful of one over the other could easily skew your perspective when not considered as part of a larger whole.

As such, you are going to want to make a point of racking the date and time you placed each trade, trade details, how you choose the trade, the financial details of the trade, your emotional state as the trade was occurring the length of time the penny stock was held for and the final results of the trade. Fastidiously keeping track of your trades is different than pouring over your results each night, however, and indeed you should plan on not checking your initial results for as long as a month to ensure that you are taking advantage of a large enough sample size. The only exception to this is if paying careful attention to your experiences as they happen has indicated to you that your success rate is somewhere south of 25 percent, in this case you can dig into your results after two weeks in an effort to determine what has gone wrong.

When you do get around to checking your stats, it is crucial that you maintain a realistic stance on what the results of a successful trade looks like to prevent yourself from feeling the need to tinker with a plan that is already on the right track. Specifically, this means you will want to strive to find a plan that has a success rate of at least 60 percent, though anything above 50 is acceptable. If this is the case they you are virtually guaranteed to turn a profit in a long run, even if it may not feel like it in the moment.

Chapter 3:
Trading Styles to Consider

When it comes to trading in penny stocks that are numerous different ways to go about doing so while still making a tidy profit. As such, it is important to experiment with multiple different variations to ensure you have found the one that is the best fit for you before you settle into a trading routine to truly focus on. Even if the first method you try seems effective it is important to continue to broaden your skillset as you never know what trading style might be waiting for you over the next horizon. There are three main styles of penny stock trading that are currently in use, with the first, a variation of traditional day trading being the most popular on average.

Day trading: Regardless of what market they are working in, day traders are known for making money as quickly as they can and rarely if ever holding onto a position overnight. If you are interested in this type of trading, then you will typically be trading the trends of the stocks in question as opposed to whatever their underlying value might be. As the valuation that an individual penny stock company might have is just as likely to be mostly smoke and mirrors as it is to provide any real value, avoiding dealing in value prevents you from being taken to the cleaners by faulty data. Unlike value which is subjective, following the trends will give you a clear idea of the current state of things as it stands in the moment and each and every day will bring new trades to follow.

When it comes to trading in penny stocks, the most common measurement of value that you are looking for is rapid price movement in either direction to the tune of more than 30 percent of its total value multiple times per day. These are what are known as cycles and if you learn to look for them you can predict with relative certainty the movement that a specific stock is going to experience in a specific period of time. Each morning should then be spent looking for stocks that moved this amount during the evening hours as this is likely the first indicator that a cycle is about to repeat itself.

You will know that you are on the right track with the cycle you are tracking when you can trace it back to multiple clear high and low points over the previous few days. Once you have identified several cycles you can then take note of the patterns of the low points among them as an idea of what a potential future buy-in point might look like. Likewise, the pattern found in the high points will give you a good idea of where you may want to set a stop loss in the future. Day traders will follow this same pattern for several different stocks throughout the day, monitoring them closely throughout. Following this pattern for each stock that you are interested in will allow you to profit from the excessive confidence that other traders have in a current trend lasting far longer than it has historically time and again in prior incarnations.

Taking a moderate stand when it comes to the cycles of penny stocks is often considered the safest choice as the extra volatility and risk that they come with is already enough to push them out of the radar of the most risk-adverse traders. While those who let their trades ride for longer will occasionally see much larger returns overall, they are also sure to see more losses, something that is rarely going to be the right choice for most traders. Finally, you will want to keep in mind that if you are planning on following through on cycles later in the day you need to be sure that the cycle has previously persisted for more than a day in total to ensure you aren't looking for something that no longer exists.

Value trading: Whereas day traders make trades based on existing trends that determine a penny stock's current popularity, value traders are more interested in stocks that have solid fundamentals that have not yet been reflected in its price. As an example, if a company currently has a million-dollar market cap but has an asset that is projected to be worth ten million dollars in the next year then this stock is currently undervalued and it doesn't matter if it goes up and down in the interim, eventually it is going to be worth more than you paid for it. As a rule, value traders tend to go all in when they do find a penny stock that meets their qualifications as they are typically few and far between.

Value trading may be right for you if you are interested in really getting to the bottom of the companies that you invest in, digging into their financial reports and plans for the future. While many traders feel as though value trading is a better proposition in larger exchanges, those larger exchanges are also prone to more misinformation that has been spread by those with a personal interest in the outcome. On the other hand, smaller companies are going to have fewer avenues of information flowing outward which means a smaller overall flow of information to sift through and a generally improved chance of finding the right information as a result.

Remember, if you go down this route it is important to not only look for penny stocks that are undervalued, they must be undervalued and more than a handful of people need to be aware of it. If the company isn't getting any traction in the media or online, then your investment is likely to stagnate and you won't see much of a return even as the stock continues to remain undervalued. As such, this type of investment strategy can best be thought of as somewhat more long term than that of a more traditional day trading strategy.

Buy and hold trading: If value traders are more interested in the long term than day traders, buy and hold traders are even father along that same spectrum. For that reason, buy and hold traders are much the same as value traders except they only look for profits in the extreme long term. These types of traders are interested in looking for new companies that show compelling signs of making something of themselves somewhere further down the line. This type of trading is naturally suited to penny stocks as virtually all of the companies listed are going to be in a fledgling state with nothing but the potential for growth ahead of them.

If you are interested in practicing this type of trading with penny stocks, then the best course of action is to limit yourself to a single field and then learn everything you can about the state of the field today. As many as 90 percent of all penny stocks ultimately end up delisted, so this means that you are going to want to cast a wide net in order to guarantee some level of success. Once you learn all that you can you are then going to want to pick out as many promising businesses in your chosen field that you can find before only investing one percent of your total investment capital in each of them.

Once the investment has been made, it mostly becomes a waiting game. As previously noted, a majority of the companies that you invest in will ultimately end in a loss, some will maintain a stagnant growth rate and the remaining few will generate a profit. Depending on the rate of returns you are seeing you can then use some of these profits to reinvest in a large share of the growing company or redistribute them into other businesses depending on your goals and time frame. All told, these types of investments do not do good with micromanaging and are most successful if you apply a set it and forget it mentality. Finally, above all else it is important to never get too attached to a specific stock when using this trading style as overcommitting to the wrong stock is the most surefire way to skew the results in an extremely unprofitable fashion.

Chapter 4:
Fundamental Analysis

Once you have created a trading plan and chosen a complimentary trading style, the next thing that you are going to want to consider when it comes to choosing penny stock investments successfully is how you are going to gather data to determine which penny stocks you are going to want to go pursue closely and which you are going to want to give a wide berth. While there are plenty of so-called experts hawking surefire ways to tell good penny stocks from bad, the truth of the matter is that there are only two main ways to go about doing so, fundamental analysis and technical analysis and the details for each will take up the next two chapters. Technical analysis focuses almost exclusively on the current price of the stock in question because it assumes that the current price factors in everything else that is relevant to the penny stock while fundamental analysis delves into the details of the underlying company.

The primary tenants of fundamental analysis state that the whole story of a particular stock can be found if you dig deep enough while technical analysis believes that market movement provides you with all of the details that you need to know. Of the two, it is recommended that new traders start with fundamental analysis before moving on to technical analysis as, while it requires plenty of research, all of the underlying concepts at play are going to be straightforward and easy for almost anyone to understand. The biggest downside of fundamental analysis is that it can often be quite time intensive and once you have looked into the historical precedent you are often stymied by the fact that new relevant information is frequently only released a few times per year. On the other hand, technical analysis can often be completed quite quickly, especially by those who have experience in the field, though it can take a significant amount of study before the concepts at play in this type of analysis become readily apparent.

Performing fundamental analysis

When using fundamental analysis, you are looking to the past to determine the most likely future with the end result of determining the best point to jump onto a new penny stock. When getting started, you are going to want to find all of the information on the penny stock company you are interested in investing in. Once you have everything you need you will want to consider the following:

Establish a baseline: In order to begin analyzing the fundamentals, the first thing that you will need to do is to create a baseline regarding the company's overall performance. In order to generate the most useful results possible, the first thing that you are going to need to do is gather data both regarding the company in question as well as the related industry as a whole. When gathering macro data, it is important to keep in mind that no market is going to operate in a vacuum which means the reasons behind specific market movement can be much more far reaching than they first appear. Fundamental analysis works because of the stock market's propensity for patterns which means if you trace a specific market movement back to the source you will have a better idea of what to keep an eye on in the future.

Furthermore, all industries go through several different phases where their penny stocks are going to be worth more or less overall based on general popularity. If the industry is producing many popular penny stocks, then overall volatility will be down while at the same time liquidity will be at an overall high. As this level of popularity cannot be sustained indefinitely, things will eventually move into a bust period where volatility increases as liquidity decreases.

Consider worldwide issues: Once you have a general grasp on the current phase you are dealing with, the next thing you will want to consider is anything that is going on in the wider world that will after the type of businesses you tend to favor in your penny stocks. Not being prepared for major paradigm shifts, especially in penny stocks where new companies come and go so quickly, means that you can easily miss out on massive profits and should be avoided at all costs.

To ensure you are not blindsided by news you could have seen coming, it is important to look beyond the obvious issues that are consuming the 24-hour news cycle and dig deeper into the comings and goings of the nations that are going to most directly affect your particular subsection of penny stocks. One important worldwide phenomenon that you will want to pay specific attention to is anything in the realm of technology as major paradigm shifts like the adoption of the smartphone, or the current move towards electric cars, can create serious paradigm shifts that can last for multiple years until the technology is completely assimilated.

Look for historical precedents: Once you have a firm grasp on the present and a hypothetical grasp on the future you are going to need to look to the past to see how it measures up. Looking back to how the industry you are considering has done historically will give you a better idea of the true strength of the current phase. When things are starting to look up you can expect that credit will become easier to come by and erratic market movement is at a relative low which means it should be quite easy to turn a profit in nearly all sectors. This will only continue for so long, however, and the longer it does so the more likely it will be to teeter towards a bust at any moment. Remember, this is not a question of if things will turn around once more, but when they will do so.

Look into volatility: When it comes to determining the likely level of volatility that a new company is going to exhibit, the best place to look is to related penny stocks in the same general category. The lower the risk that ancillary stocks exhibit, the lower the chance that the new stock will exhibit aberrant behavior. A lower chance doesn't mean no chance, however, and as a rule of thumb it is important to always assume that volatility could spike, just to be safe. When it comes to penny stocks, planning for the worst and hoping for the best is often the most reliable way to turn a profit. A good barometer for such is the current price when compared to the phase and the current state as compared to the historical point when a bust phase is the most likely to occur.

Trade at the right times: When the time comes to experience a growth phase from the start, the best way to take advantage of it to the fullest is to start with penny stock companies that have the most reliable fundamentals possible. Penny stocks that are already more likely to be viable are going to naturally be a good choice during boom phases as they are statistically more likely to yield positive returns. They also remain a good choice if you are in a bust phase as they are likely going to still be sold for higher rates when compared with assets that are weaker overall.

Chapter 5:
Technical Analysis

When it comes to technical analysis, the most important thing to keep in mind is that it is only useful because of its belief in the fact that price movement in the past is a reliable indicator of price movement in the future. Unlike fundamental analysis, however, you don't need to wait for specific information to be released as there is already more technical data out there then you could ever hope to make it through by yourself. This overload of information can then be parsed with the help of indicators, charts and trends to ensure that you never go into a trade without having a strong reason to assume that it is going to end in a profit.

While some of what is described below will likely sound downright arcane, when it gets right down to it what you are shooting for is to find strong future trends. Give it some time, and with practice you will be reading technical charts with the best of them.

The basics: First and foremost, technical analysis lives and dies based on what it can measure of a particular trade based on its similarity to a previous pattern that has not yet become apparent to a large number of people. If you hope to be successful when it comes to using technical analysis you will want to do your best to ensure three things are true for the best results. First, the market is bound to discount everything at some point. Second, price and trends are connected which means one is always an indicator of the other. Finally, history will always repeat itself when given a long enough timeline.

It is because of these three tenants that proponents of technical analysis to conclude that the current price a given stock is going for is the only metric of note as it is an amalgamation of everything that is going on in the world that affects the stock in question. What this means is that as long as you know the current price of the stock you are interested in then you have access to all the details on the current economic climate as a whole. This is relevant as technical analysis also posits that all prices move according to a variety of different trends that have already been catalogued which means all you need to do is to find the right one and you can accurately predict what the penny stock in question is going to do next.

While this might sound a little presumptive, it is really just a function of the fact that there are so many stocks to too choose from and that it is much more likely for a previous pattern to repeat itself than it is for an entirely new pattern to be spontaneously generated, especially when there is so much historical stock data that is already readily available. When this relative inevitability is then combined with the fact that humans are naturally attracted to patterns, it creates a powerful metric that not only explains what a trend is likely going to mean for the stock in which you have spotted it, but it can also tell you what your competition is likely to do about it. Again, if this sounds unlikely consider the fact that several of the first technical analysis patterns that were first discovered more than 100 years ago, are still currently in use today.

Pinpoint the trend: Understanding what trend means for a potential penny stock trade is going to be a crucial skill to master if you hope to find success in the long term. While ideally you will be looking for the strongest trends you can find, it is important to keep in mind that they run the gamut from weak to strong with some being faint enough to be completely irrelevant and others being so strong that they are impossible for almost anyone to miss. It is important to keep this fact in mind and always do your due diligence to look for existing patterns while also being careful to not attribute meaning to patterns that do not actually exist.

The best way to ensure what you are seeing is really there is to seek out a collection of highs and lows that are clustered together in a large enough grouping to show that a pattern exists beyond a shadow of a doubt. Cutting out the middle static of a given pattern will likely make it much easier to determine its overall level of usefulness. This is not to say that a pattern is likely to be all highs or all lows, instead you will know that you are on the right track if you see a number of highs topping previous highs, known as an uptrend; or lows following previous lows, known as a reversal. If you find a pattern that has more or less an equal number of both highs and lows, then what you have identified is known as a horizontal trend.

When you find a trend that appears to last longer with each cycle, then what you can reasonably expect is that the next cycle will also be longer, while at the same time being prepared for the inevitable reversal. When you come across a trend that appears to be quite short, the first thing that you are going to want to do is ensure that it is not part of some longer trend that you are just not seeing. The best way to do this is to look at a longer stretch of charts and see if anything comes of it. While this can make the process take much longer than it otherwise might, it is important to ensure you are not acting on incomplete information. The same can be said about switching to charts of a shorter time frame as looking at trends under a microscope can allow them to make sense out of otherwise incomprehensible information.

Map it: Once you have found the trend you think you are looking for, the next step is going to be creating a trendline as a way of qualifying what it is that you have found. To do this all you need to do is place a straight line through the data points you are curious about, specifically the high points for a negative trend and the low points for a positive trend. What you will have created is then known as a resistance line and it is a physical representation of the market's ability to push back on the penny stock in question whenever it gets cither too high or too low. While not always useful when it comes to predicting what the stock in question is going to do next, it will tell you the overall limits of how the stock is likely to move.

Once you are finished drawing the primary line, the next thing you will need to do is to draw a line on either side of the primary trend line to show ancillary levels of resistance and support. This channel will then either move positively, negatively or horizontally. If you extend this channel to a long enough point, then you should be able to determine where the price is likely to split from the norm which indicates the period when you will likely need to act if you want to generate the maximum profit possible.

Chapter 6:
Tips and Tricks

Focus on liquidity: While liquidity is always a concern when investing in a securities market, there are few places where it will more drastically come into play than when you are dealing with penny stocks no matter the exchange, specifically if you are planning to practice day trading. Liquidity can be thought of as a function of spread which, in turn, can be thought of as the difference between what the stock is currently selling for and what it is currently being purchased for or is estimated to be selling for at a point in the future.

This difference stems from the fact that a majority of the stock that is bought or sold each day is sold by brokerages rather than individuals or the companies themselves which means that the rate at which the stock is sold can vary dramatically, even in a particularly short period of time. As a rule, the greater the spread, the more difficulty you will have moving the stock in question when the time comes to do something with it besides just hang on and hope for the best. When you are working with penny stocks you are in the relatively unique position in that the spread you are looking at can sometimes get to the point where there is practically no way you can ever expect to sell the stock in question.

When it comes to day trading, you will often find the best result if you keep a tight spread to your trades and only stick to penny stocks whose underlying companies have a market cap that is at least two million dollars. While holding on to a penny stock when it is on a strong upswing can be tempting, the right move here is to sell after you have seen enough positive movement to make it worth your while as it is likely not a question of if the stock is going to turn back around but when. Selling from a reasonable point on the spectrum will allow you to avoid the problems that might develop if the spread gets too large.

When it comes to other trading styles you will find that liquidity is less of a factor as it loses practically all of its relevance when you leave the short term and start looking at broader swathes of time. Regardless, it is important to stick with companies who have a valuation that is greater than $500,000 at the very least.

Pay special attention to volatility: Another one of penny stocks' biggest strengths is the high degree of volatility that the marketplace is likely to experience in a given period of time. In this instance, volatility can be thought of as the amount of change that a given stock is likely to undergo over a set period of time. When it comes to day trading you are going to want to look for volatility of greater than 30 percent within anywhere from 6 to 8 hours in a single day. Assuming it is an average day you should be able to find anywhere from 4 to 8 stocks that meet this qualification with minimal issues. The absolute minimum level of volatility that you can safely move forward with is a slim 10 percent as any less means that a majority of your profits are going to be eaten up by fees associated with placing the order in the first place.

Trade in the right places: When it comes to trading penny stocks, you are likely going to have the most success looking in the New York Stock Exchange (NYSE) and the Over the

Counter Bulletin Board. There are many other smaller exchanges that you can find which sell all manner of penny stocks but these two typically offer the best mix of price and quality. While the NYSE is more famous for major stocks, it also offers its own separate exchange dedicated to penny stocks that trade somewhere between $1 and $5. While it often costs a little more to purchase penny stocks through the NYSE, in exchange you can trade with more confidence than many penny stocks offer as the vetting process for these stocks is stricter than many of its competitors. This level of confidence is extremely important in the penny stock world as many exchanges make it much easier to allow companies to misrepresent themselves to investors.

Of the various main exchanges where trading penny stocks occurs, you will find that the most useful if you are planning to practice day trading is the OTCBB. While the NYSE might have the highest reputation for quality, the OTCBB is where traders go when then need to move stock as quickly as possible as it has a greater degree of infrastructure which gets more trades in front of more people in the shortest period of time possible. Finding the best deals is then just a matter of finding the most active stocks out of the bunch.

Have the right mindset: When it comes to trading on the regular it is important to have a plan, but it is equally important that you know how to stick to your plan no matter what. In order to cultivate this ideal mindset, it is important that you focus on improving four key attributes. The first of these attributes is patience as it can take a goodly amount of time for the right circumstances to materialize around a given stock after you have determined the ideal entry or exit point. Trading stocks, especially penny stocks, is a waiting game and the sooner you get comfortable with that fact the more successful you will be. Remember, once you are already in the midst of a trade there is nothing to be gained by changing either your exit or your entry points so it is best to no focus on what might go wrong and instead focus on everything you can do to swing the odds in your favor.

If you have done the work to ensure that you know the players in your chosen field back to front, followed that up with research on the stock that you are currently considering purchasing and strengthened your odds by learning more about the theory behind the type of trading that you prefer, then it is only natural that all of this faith would pay off. Don't overthink it, you created the system that takes the conditions of the stocks you favor into account and you have the chance to profit from them, but only if you believe in yourself and the system that you have created.

This does not mean that you do not need to be objective, however, as it is important to work to improve your objectivity whenever possible as well. While external factors can do some of the work, you will always find that the best trades are those that qualify for your system, period. If you listen to anything other than what your system is telling you then you are letting other people dictate your movements instead of determining them for yourself. Learn to evaluate each trade based on its own merits and then learn to trust that you have objectively made the right decision.

Finally, it is important that prior to making any trade you have a clear idea of what you can expect the end result to be. Measured expectations are key to long term success as if you let your expectations get out of hand then you are already one step closer to giving in to your emotions which is more likely than not going to lead to big losses and often sooner than you might expect. A good rule of thumb is that shorter trades are typically considered safer while long-term trades can lead to bigger rewards. Knowing the risk that comes along with every potential reward will make it easier for you to stick to your system in the long run.

Set trading limits: While understanding that risk is the key to reward might seem pretty straight forward, putting this thought into action can easily be more difficult than it first appears. As such, especially early on, you will likely find that you have better overall results when you limit the amount of loss that you can experience in a single day before taking a timeout and giving yourself the time you need to ensure you are not on an emotional tilt. Even if it doesn't appear to be the case at the time, the truth of the matter is that experiencing a steady stream of losses will affect how you analyze future opportunities which is why it is important to reset every now and then to ensure you are interpreting the data that you are seeing in the correct fashion.

As a good rule of thumb, it is best to go ahead and take the rest of the day off when you find that you are down a full 10 percent of the entirety of your trading capital. Remember, the results of your plan don't need to be close to 100 percent in order for you to turn a real profit, all you need is 60 percent or better to ensure a solid return on your investment. As such, it is only natural to experience loss on a regular basis which means it is crucial that you learn how to deal with it properly to ensure that it does not compound upon itself each time it occurs. Sometimes there really is nothing you can do except to wait for the market to be in a better mood.

Know when to go off book: When it comes to trading successfully, one of the best pieces of advice that you can learn to follow is to trade like a robot. This means to keep your emotions out of the equation and do nothing but trade the stocks your plan says are the best bet. However, there will inevitably come a time when the circumstances of the market change drastically enough in a short enough period of time that your plan is no longer valid in its current form. It is important that you be aware of this fact and make it a point to never stick with your plan just to stick with it, and to instead only stick to the plan as long as it continues to seem like the best possible course of action.

Part and parcel with this is understanding the current mood of the market. It doesn't matter what type of analysis that you favor, you are still going to need to consider what the other traders around you are currently thinking based on what you can see that they are doing. This can be seen most clearly in the major players in your chosen field, keeping an eye on them should provide you with a clear idea of the temperature of the market without requiring you to do too much extra work to get the inside scoop. Even better, you will then have a distinct advantage over all of those who did not take the time to do the same.

Don't feel as though you have to trade: One of the biggest mistakes that many new traders make is feeling as though they must always be trading or else they are doing something wrong. The truth of the matter is that trading too often can be even worse than not trading enough for when you are not trading enough all you are doing is missing out on potential profit while if you are trading too much you are running the risk of not only missing out on profits but actually losing money as well. While it might be hard to believe, you can easily get by on a very small number of trades as long as they are the right trades. It is a very literal case where quality will trump quantity every single time.

Chapter 7:
Mistakes to Avoid

Not taking the right message from trades that end poorly: While it might be hard to internalize properly, no one trades with a 100 percent success rate with any degree of reliability. This doesn't mean that there aren't lessons to be learned from every failed trade, however, and it is important to look back on each after the fact and ensure that you stuck to your plan no matter what. As long as this is the case, then you have done right by the trade, even when it does not work out to the end. If you ever hope to truly trade successfully then it is important to separate the end result of a trade from your performance in said trade and analyze both separately to ensure the best results.

Choosing a broker at random: With so many things to consider, it is easy to understand why many new penny stock traders simply settle on the first broker that they find and go about their business from there. The fact of the matter is, however, that the broker you choose is going to be a huge part of your overall trading experience which means that the importance of choosing the right one should not be discounted if you are hoping for the best experience possible. This means that the first thing that you are going to want to do is to dig past the friendly exterior of their website and get to the meat and potatoes of what it is they truly offer. Remember, creating an eye-catching website is easy, filling it will legitimate information when you have ill intent is much more difficult.

First things first, this means looking into their history of customer service as a way of not only ensuring that they treat their customers in the right way, but also of checking to see that quality of service is where it needs to be as well. Remember, when you make a trade every second counts which means that if you need to contact your broker for help with a trade you need to know that you are going to be speaking with a person who can solve your problem as quickly as possible. The best way to ensure the customer service is up to snuff is to give them a call and see how long it takes for them to get back to you. If you wait more than a single business day, take your business elsewhere as if they are this disinterested in a new client, consider what the service is going to be like when they already have you right where they want you.

With that out the way, the next thing you will need to consider is the fees that the broker is going to charge in exchange for their services. There is very little regulation when it comes to these fees which means it is definitely going to pay to shop around. In addition to fees, it is important to consider any account minimums that are required as well as any fees having to do with withdrawing funds from the account. At the same time, be sure to keep any eye out for any additional benefits that might come with the account including things like free classes to enhance your skills.

Trying to make do with old technology: While taking your first steps into being a penny stock trader doesn't mean that you automatically need to go out and spend $2,000 or more on a new computer, it does mean that the technology you are using matters. As the most common way that penny stocks are traded is via day trading, it is important to consider what type of technology your competition is going to be using and then work to be in the same league, if not in the same ballpark.

This means you are going to want to have a computer that is up to the task as well as a video card that can handle at least two, if not three monitors. Additionally, you will want to have a backup internet connection just in case your primary connection goes down. While this might sound like an extravagance now, it will only take one use of it to complete a crucial trade which a given stock is in the money for it to pay for itself. Along these same lines, invest in a landline just in case everything goes down and the only recourse you have is to call your broker on the telephone. Remember, may penny stock trades are going to hinge on having split second timing, don't hamstring yourself by making do with a single laptop from the start of the decade, sometimes you really do need to spend money in order to make money.

Choose the wrong moment to get in on the action: During the early days of your trading career it is perfectly natural to feel overwhelmed from time to time which means that when you see an ongoing trend it can seem like a good idea to jump on it now and then ask questions about the specifics once the smoke clears. While you are sure to get lucky from time to time, the fact of the matter is that trends are only as good as the patterns they are a part of. Remember, the earlier that you get in on an emerging trend the more likely you are to profit from the movement that it generates. As such, if you spot a trend that is just about to peak, it is better to do your research and wait to get in on the next round of the cycle rather than jumping in at a point where you put yourself at risk for a loss, especially when you have no data with which to infer when it is coming.

Failing to balance research with what is going on in front of them: Research is an important part of a successful career trading any stocks, and penny stocks in particular. This doesn't mean that it is the end all and be all when it comes to making good trading decisions, however, as it is important that you always take your historical data with a grain of salt when compared with the current state of things. Remember, public sentiment is oftentimes just as important, if not even more so that what the research tells you and one of the things that separates novice traders from the experts is their ability to blend their research with the current state of things in order to determine where the two intersect at the current point in time.

On the other hand, traders who lean too heavily on public opinion while not taking the historical data into account can often make the right decision in the moment without then knowing how to back it up with the correct next step moving forward. Not taking the time to know if the current price is above or below the historical average means taking a risk on everything from potential profits to potential losses and is likely to work out just as poorly, if not even worse, than waiting around and doing nothing.

Not getting serious: When it comes to ensuring that you find success while trading penny stocks it is important to treat the entire experience like a job from the very first trade that you make. Remember, you are not just competing against the market as whole, you are competing against every other penny stock trader out there which means if you hope to more than throw your money away on fly by night companies you are going to need to get serious. What this means is trading at the same time each and every day, and committing to be up and at it each morning before the market opens doing your research to ensure you are not going in blind.

Furthermore, if you are treating penny stock trading like a job then this means you are going to be your own boss. This, in turn, means that you are going to need to look down deep inside yourself and find the strength and dedication to do the hard thing and dedicate yourself to the success you hope to find. More specifically, this means that in most cases when you have an active trade on the table you are going to want to glue yourself to the screen and not blink for even a second. The fact that you are sitting in your home staring at numbers on a screen that correspond to companies you have never heard of can easily start to make the entire experience feel surreal. This feeling will quickly dissipate, however, the second that you go to make yourself a sandwich only to find out that your current sure thing trade suddenly dropped out of the money while you weren't looking. Do yourself a favor and treat trading like a job and it will, in turn, reward you as if it was one.

Conclusion

Thank for making it through to the end of *Penny Stocks: A Quick and Easy Guide for Beginners to Start Investing*, let's hope it was informative and able to provide you with all of the tools you need to achieve your goals, whatever it is that they may be. Just because you've finished this book doesn't mean there is nothing left to learn on the topic, expanding your horizons is the only way to find the mastery you seek and earn the riches that you so justly deserve.

The next step is to stop reading already and to start creating your personalized trading plan before going on to research the first round of penny stock companies that catch your eye. Remember, trading in theory is different than trading in practice which means that it is perfectly natural if your first dozen or so trades don't go exactly as planned. While you might be tempted to try trading with fake money before moving on to the real thing, the fact of the matter is that this type of training doesn't accurately mimic the mental state of real trading which means that it is likely going to be of minimal good in your quest to become a better trader.

Instead, the most beneficial course of action is to practice with a very small amount of money first, to provide you with the opportunity to trade when the stakes are real, while at the same time ensuring your trading career is not over before it begins because of a little bit of performance anxiety. While it can be easy to get overwhelmed, if you take things one trade at a time, and always keep detailed notes, then you will find that you are marking down more positive trades than negative ones sooner than you might think. From there it is only a matter of keeping up the good work and reaping the rewards that you so justly deserve.